BABYnouveau™
~Stylish Blankets for Baby~

Amy Polcyn

HOUSE of
WHITE
BIRCHES
PUBLISHERS
SINCE 1947

Table of Contents

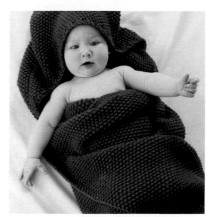

Introduction

Baby blankets make perfect gifts; you don't have to worry about fit or sizing and no new parent can have too many. These 10 designs offer a range of techniques to try, from mosaic colorwork to lace to brioche knitting. For the brand-new knitter, there are several options that require no more than knowing how to cast on, bind off and do the knit stitch. All of the yarns suggested (ranging from DK to super bulky weight) are machine washable, and many are machine dryable as well for easy care. Two sizes are provided for some of the designs—both for full-size baby blankets and smaller travel-size blankets to use in the car or on the go. Several designs knit in super bulky yarns make perfect play mats and provide more cushioning and comfort than a traditional blanket when baby is playing on the floor.

Helpful Hints

For ease in working with larger numbers of stitches, use at least a 24-inch-long circular needle to work back and forth in rows. This will help support the piece in your lap and make for more comfortable knitting. When working repeats of a stitch pattern, consider using stitch markers to separate each repeat; this will make it easier to keep track of the pattern and correct mistakes quickly. Want to adjust the size? For most of the designs in this book, it's as simple as adding extra stitch repeats (be sure to change the cast-on amount), working the piece longer or, easier still, working the borders longer and wider. Although gauge is listed for each pattern, it's not essential that it be matched exactly. In a hurry? The bulkier play-mat patterns can be whipped up in a day.

Amy Polcyn

Amy Polcyn

Mosaic Chains

Get the look of stranded colorwork without the hassle! This pattern uses just one color at a time with no long floats that could get tangled in baby's fingers.

Skill Level

◼◼◼◻ INTERMEDIATE

Finished Size
30 x 34 inches

Materials
- Cascade 220 Superwash (worsted weight; 100% superwash wool; 220 yds/100g per skein): 3 skeins pink rose #835 (A) and 2 skeins citron #886 (B)
- Size 7 (4.5mm) 29-inch circular needle or size needed to obtain gauge
- Size 6 (4mm) 29-inch circular needle

4 MEDIUM

Gauge
23 sts and 34 rows = 4 inches/10cm in Mosaic Chains pat with larger needle.

To save time, take time to check gauge.

Pattern Notes
Blanket is worked back and forth; a circular needle is used to accommodate the large number of stitches—do not join.

Slip all stitches purlwise.

Work in 1 color only for each group of 2 rows (Rows 1 and 2, Rows 3 and 4, etc). The slipped stitches will create the color pattern. Each wrong-side row is worked the same as the previous right-side row, purling the stitches knit in the previous row in the same color and slipping the same stitches as were slipped in the previous row.

Carry the unused color loosely up the side.

Pattern Stitch
Mosaic Chains (multiple of 8 sts + 2)
Note: Chart is provided for those preferring to work Mosaic Chains pat from a chart.
Row 1 (RS): With B, k3, sl 1, k2, sl 1, *k4, sl 1, k2, sl 1; rep from * to last 3 sts, k3.
Row 2: With B, p3, sl 1, p2, sl 1, *p4, sl 1, p2, sl 1; rep from * to last 3 sts, p3.
Row 3: With A, k1, sl 1, k2, *sl 2, k2; rep from * to last 2 sts, sl 1, k1.
Row 4: With A, p1, sl 1, p2, *sl 2, p2; rep from * to last 2 sts, sl 1, p1.
Rows 5 and 6: With B, rep Rows 1 and 2.
Row 7: With A, k2, *sl 1, k4, sl 1, k2; rep from * to end.
Row 8: With A, p2, *sl 1, p4, sl 1, p2; rep from * to end.
Rows 9 and 10: With B, rep Rows 3 and 4.
Rows 11 and 12: With A, rep Rows 7 and 8.
Rep Rows 1–12 for pat.

Blanket
With smaller needle and A, cast on 146 sts.

Work in garter st for 2 inches, ending with a RS row.

Change to larger needle.

Next row (WS): With A, purl across.

Work in Mosaic Chains pat until piece measures approx 32 inches.

With A, work in garter st for 2 inches.

Bind off.

Side Borders
Pick-up row (RS): With RS facing, smaller needle and A, pick up and knit approx 1 st per ridge along side of garter borders and 2 sts for every 3 rows of stockinette section.

Work in garter st for 2 inches.

Bind off.

Rep on opposite side.

Finishing
Weave in ends. Block as desired. ●

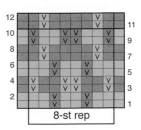

STITCH KEY

▉	With A, k on RS, p on WS
▨	With B, k on RS, p on WS
V	Sl 1, carrying color indicated into next row

MOSAIC CHAINS

Coloblock Quilt

This blanket has the look of a patchwork quilt without the work! Simple bands of garter stitch build up from the center out in coordinating colors.

....

Skill Level

■□□□ BEGINNER

Finished Sizes
Travel (full) Instructions are given for smaller size, with larger size in parentheses. When only 1 number is given, it applies to both sizes.

Finished Measurements
22 (32) inches x 29 (39) inches

Materials

- Classic Elite Sprout (chunky weight; 100% organic cotton; 109 yds/100g per hank): 2 (3) hanks smokey lavender #4305 (A), 1 (2) hank(s) summer rain #4375 (B) and 2 hanks summer cloud #4301 (C)
- Size 10½ (6.5mm) 29-inch circular needle or size needed to obtain gauge

Gauge
13 sts and 24 rows = 4 inches/10cm in garter st.

To save time, take time to check gauge.

Pattern Notes
Blanket is worked back and forth; a circular needle is used to accommodate the large number of stitches—do not join.

Slip the first stitch of each row purlwise.

When picking up stitches along edge, pick up 1 stitch in each slipped-stitch chain or 1 stitch in each stitch across.

Work the sections longer or shorter than indicated to customize the look and size of the finished blanket.

Blanket

Center Block
With A, cast on 46 sts.

Work in garter st, slipping the first st of each row pwise, until piece measures 8 inches.

Bind off.

Section 1
Turn piece so that side edge is at top.

With RS facing and C, pick up and knit 24 sts along edge.

Work in garter st as before for 3 inches.

Bind off.

Rep on opposite short edge of center block.

Section 2
Turn piece so that long edge of center block is at top.

With RS facing and B, pick up and knit 64 sts along edge, including sides of section 1.

Work in garter st as before for 3 inches.

Bind off.

Rep on opposite edge of center block.

Section 3
Turn piece so that short edge is at top.

With RS facing and A, pick up and knit 42 sts along edge.

Work in garter st as before for 4 inches.

Bind off.

Rep on opposite edge.

Section 4

Turn piece so that long edge is at top.

With RS facing and C, pick up and knit 84 sts along edge.

Work in garter st as before for 4 inches.

Bind off.

Rep on opposite edge.

Travel size is complete.

Continue with Finishing.

Section 5
For Full size only

Turn piece so that short edge is at top.

With RS facing and B, pick up and knit 64 sts along edge.

Work in garter st as before for 5 inches.

Bind off.

Rep on opposite edge.

Section 6
For Full size only

Turn piece so that long edge is at top.

With RS facing and A, pick up and knit 108 sts along edge.

Work in garter st as before for 5 inches.

Bind off.

Rep on opposite edge.

Continue with Finishing.

Finishing
Weave in ends. Block lightly. ●

Simple Squares

A perfect project for a brand-new knitter, simple squares of stockinette are knit, then arranged checkerboard style, alternating knit and purl sides. It's quick, easy and perfect for on-the-go knitting.

· ·

Skill Level

 BEGINNER

Finished Sizes
Travel (full) Instructions are given for smaller size, with larger size in parentheses. When only 1 number is given, it applies to both sizes.

Finished Measurements
23 (38) inches square

Materials
- Schaefer Yarn Chris (worsted weight; 80% extra fine superwash merino wool/20% nylon; 215 yds/113g per skein): 2 (6) skeins Annie
- Size 7 (4.5mm) needles or size needed to obtain gauge
- Size 7 (4.5mm) crochet hook

4 MEDIUM

Gauge
18 sts and 24 rows = 4 inches/10cm in St st.

To save time, take time to check gauge.

Pattern Notes
For Travel size, very little yarn is left over. If you run short, try using a small amount of a leftover yarn in a contrasting color to work the joining.

This project also works perfectly as a "stash" buster—gather up an assortment of leftover machine washable worsted-weight yarns and knit the squares in different colors, make stripes and have fun!

Blanket

Squares
Make 9 (25)

Cast on 34 sts.

Work in St st for 7½ inches.

Bind off.

Finishing
Block squares to make joining easier.

Arrange in a checkerboard fashion, alternating knit and purl sides facing as shown, in 3 rows of 3 squares (5 rows of 5 squares).

With crochet hook and sc, join squares into strips, allowing the seams to show on the RS. Once all strips are complete, join the strips using sc.

Edging
With RS facing, join yarn and work 1 rnd of sc around the outside edge of blanket. Fasten off.

Weave in ends. Block again lightly. ●

Magnificent Miters

An oversized mitered square worked in two colors of variegated yarn creates a deliciously complex look with minimum effort.

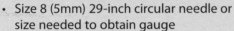

Skill Level
 EASY

Finished Size
38 inches square

Materials
- Jojoland Rhythm Superwash (worsted weight; 100% wool; 110 yds/ 50g per ball) 6 balls each feeling blue #RS71 (A) and martini dance #RS67 (B)
- Size 8 (5mm) 29-inch circular needle or size needed to obtain gauge
- Stitch marker

4 MEDIUM

Gauge
16 sts and 32 rows = 4 inches/10cm in garter st.

To save time, take time to check gauge.

Pattern Notes
Blanket is worked back and forth; a circular needle is used to accommodate the large number of stitches—do not join.

Alternate colors A and B every 2 rows throughout.

Slip the first st of each row purlwise throughout.

Blanket

Center Square

With A, cast on 217 sts. Place marker on center st, leaving 108 sts on either side of center st.

Row 1 (RS): Sl 1, knit to end.

Row 2: Sl 1, knit to 1 st before marked st, sk2p, knit to end—2 sts dec.

Change to B; rep Rows 1 and 2 until 3 sts rem, alternating A and B every 2 rows throughout.

Last row: K3tog—1 st.

Fasten off.

Corners

Orient square in a diamond shape, with cast-on row at the bottom.

Pick-up row (RS): With RS facing and A, pick up and knit 108 sts along one of the sides with a cast-on edge.

Row 1 (WS): Knit across.

Row 2: K2tog, knit to last 2 sts, ssk—2 sts dec.

Rep Rows 1 and 2 until 2 sts rem.

Last row: K2tog—1 st.

Fasten off.

Rep on opposite side with a cast-on edge.

Rep on 2 upper sides.

Finishing

Weave in ends. Block lightly. ●

Pinwheels

Simple stockinette stitch is brightened up with fun free-form spirals of I-cord. An applied I-cord border creates a coordinating finish. This project is another great "stash" buster—try using leftover bits of different-color yarn to make the I-cord embellishments for a more colorful look.

. . . .

Skill Level

◼◼◼◻ INTERMEDIATE

Finished Sizes
Travel (full) Instructions are given for smaller size, with larger size in parentheses. When only 1 number is given, it applies to both sizes.

Finished Measurements
24 (30) inches x 30 (36) inches

Materials
- Classic Elite/Jil Eaton Minnow Merino (worsted weight; 100% extra fine superwash merino; 77 yds/50g per hank)· 11 hanks cerise #4/55
- Size 8 (5mm) 29-inch circular and 2 double-point needles or size needed to obtain gauge

Gauge
17 sts and 24 rows = 4 inches/10cm in St st.

To save time, take time to check gauge.

Special Techniques
I-cord: With dpn, cast on 4 sts. *Slide sts to opposite end of needle, k4, do not turn; rep from * until cord is desired length. Bind off.

Applied I-cord: With dpn, cast on 4 sts. Work 1 row of I-cord, then with WS facing, pick up 1 st from edge of piece—5 sts. *Sl 5 back to RH dpn. K3, ssk (last st on dpn and picked-up st), pick up and knit another st from edge of piece; rep from * around. Skip sts or rows periodically as you pick up sts in the main fabric to keep edge from flaring (the rate at which you skip will depend on your gauge). Either bind off and sew

ends of Applied I-cord tog, or leave sts live and graft ends using Kitchener st, page 44.

Pattern Notes

Blanket is worked back and forth; a circular needle is used to accommodate the large number of stitches—do not join.

Length and number of I-cord strips is up to you! Make as few or many as you like.

Instead of spirals, try making the baby's initials or other designs as desired.

Tip: Make a large gauge swatch, then work Applied I-cord around the edge. This will help you establish the proper rate at which to pick up stitches along the edge so that the edge doesn't flare.

Blanket

Cast on 102 (126) sts.

Work in St st until piece measures 30 (36) inches.

Bind off.

Finishing

Work Applied I-cord around perimeter of blanket.

Embellishments

Work I-cords for desired length (on sample, longest piece is approx 4 feet long), making as many pieces as desired.

Arrange on blanket as desired and whipstitch in place.

Weave in ends. Block. ●

Tumbling Blocks

A texture pattern of knits and purls creates a 3-D effect of stacked blocks. The yarn, made of recycled fibers, is soft with a slightly tweedy look that adds an extra bit of depth to the design.

Skill Level

■■■□ INTERMEDIATE

Finished Sizes
Travel (full) Instructions are given for smaller size, with larger size in parentheses. When only 1 number is given, it applies to both sizes.

Finished Measurements
27 (33) inches square

Materials
- Berroco Remix (worsted weight; 100% recycled fibers: 30% nylon/ 27% cotton/24% acrylic/10% silk/ 9% linen; 216 yds/100g per ball). 4 (5) balls clementine #3924
- Size 8 (5mm) 29-inch circular needle or size needed to obtain gauge

4 MEDIUM

Gauge
18 sts and 24 rows = 4 inches/10cm in Tumbling Blocks pat.

To save time, take time to check gauge.

Pattern Stitch
Tumbling Blocks (multiple of 10 sts)
See chart.

Pattern Note
Blanket is worked back and forth; a circular needle is used to accommodate the large number of stitches—do not join.

This design is easy to customize to any size. Cast on stitches in a multiple of 10 and just follow the chart to the desired length.

Blanket
Cast on 120 (150) sts.

Work in Tumbling Blocks pat until piece measures 27 (33) inches.

Bind off.

Finishing
Weave in ends. Block lightly. ●

STITCH KEY
☐ K on RS, p on WS
⊟ P on RS, k on WS

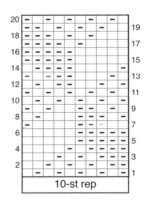

TUMBLING BLOCKS

Baby Brioche

Brioche stitch gives a thick, dimensional look to this blanket knit in cool cotton. Pair a solid with a coordinating self-striping yarn for a color pattern that looks more complex than it is.

Skill Level

◼◼◼◻ INTERMEDIATE

Sizes
Travel (full) Instructions are given for smaller size, with larger size in parentheses. When only 1 number is given, it applies to both sizes.

Finished Measurements
26 (32) inches x 32½ (37½) inches

Materials
- Universal Cotton Supreme (worsted weight; 100% cotton; 180 yds/100g per skein): 2 skeins caramel #505 (A)
- Universal Cotton Supreme Batik (worsted weight; 100% cotton; 180 yds/100g per skein): 2 (3) skeins summer camp #26 (B)
- Size 9 (5.5mm) 29-inch circular needle or size needed to obtain gauge
- Stitch markers

4 MEDIUM

Gauge
13 sts and 16 rows = 4 inches/10cm in Brioche pat.

To save time, take time to check gauge.

Special Abbreviation
Knit 1 below (k1b): Knit into center of st below next st on LH needle.

Pattern Stitch
Brioche (even number of sts)
Row 1 (WS): Knit.
Row 2: K2, place marker, *k1, k1b; rep from * to last 2 sts, place marker, k2.
Rep Row 2 for pat, slipping markers.

Pattern Note
Blanket is worked back and forth; a circular needle is used to accommodate the large number of stitches—do not join.

Blanket
With B, cast on 84 (106) sts.

Work in Brioche pat for approx 6½ (7½) inches.

Change to A and continue in Brioche pat for 6½ (7½) inches.

Continue as set, alternating colors every 6½ (7½) inches until there are a total of 5 stripes, ending with B.

Bind off somewhat firmly.

Finishing
Weave in ends. Block lightly, taking care not to flatten the sts. ●

Diagonal Stripes

Use the yarn suggested to make a thick and cushiony play mat for the floor, or use any other yarn you like. This pattern will work with ANY yarn and ANY gauge—perfect for late-night knitting emergencies when the only available yarn shopping is in your stash.

Skill Level

◐■□□ EASY

Finished Size
34 inches square or desired size

Materials
- Spud and Chloe Outer (super bulky weight; 65% superwash wool/ 35% organic cotton; 60 yds/100g per skein): 4 skeins each bayou #7207 (A) and flannel #7201 (B)
- Size 15 (10mm) 29-inch circular needle or size needed to obtain gauge

6 SUPER BULKY

Gauge
8 sts and 16 rows = 4 inches/10cm in garter st.

To save time, take time to check gauge.

Special Abbreviation
Knit in front and back (kfb): Knit in front and then in back of next st to inc 1.

Pattern Notes
Blanket is worked back and forth; a circular needle is used to accommodate the large number of stitches at the widest point—do not join.

Change colors every 16 rows throughout.

Blanket
With A, cast on 1 st.

Row 1 (WS): Kfb—2 sts.

Inc row: Kfb, knit to end.

Rep Inc row until there are 96 sts or until side edge of triangle measures 34 inches or desired width of blanket.

Dec row: K2tog, knit to end.

Rep Dec row until 1 st rem.

Fasten off.

Finishing
Weave in ends. Block lightly. ●

Swirling Lace

A delicate lace pattern swirls back and forth, creating a soothing look for baby.

Skill Level

◼◼◼◻ INTERMEDIATE

Finished Sizes
Travel (full) Instructions are given for smaller size, with larger size in parentheses. When only 1 number is given, it applies to both sizes.

Finished Measurements
24 (30) inches x 30 (36) inches

Materials
- Louet Gems Worsted (worsted weight; 100% merino wool; 175 yds/100g per skein): 4 (5) skeins goldenrod #65
- Size 7 (4.5mm) 29-Inch circular needle or size needed to obtain gauge
- Stitch markers

4 MEDIUM

Gauge
18 sts and 24 rows = 4 inches/10cm in Swirl Lace pat after blocking.

To save time, take time to check blocked gauge.

Pattern Stitches
Swirl Lace (multiple of 7 + 4 sts)
Note: Chart is provided for those preferring to work Swirl Lace pat from a chart.
Row 1 and all WS rows: Purl across.
Row 2 (RS): K3, *ssk, k5, yo; rep from * across, end k1.
Row 4: K3, *ssk, k4, yo, k1; rep from * across, end k1.
Row 6: K3, *ssk, k3, yo, k2; rep from * across, end k1.
Row 8: K3, *ssk, k2, yo, k3; rep from * across, end k1.
Row 10: K3, *ssk, k1, yo, k4; rep from * across, end k1.
Row 12: K3, *ssk, yo, k5; rep from * across, end k1.
Row 14: K1, *yo, k5, k2tog; rep from * across, end k3.
Row 16: K2, *yo, k4, k2tog, k1; rep from * across, end k2.

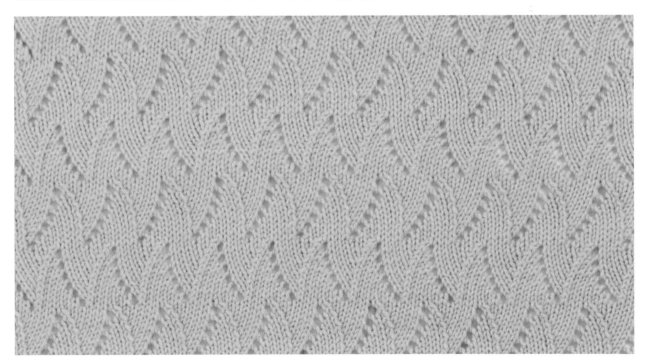

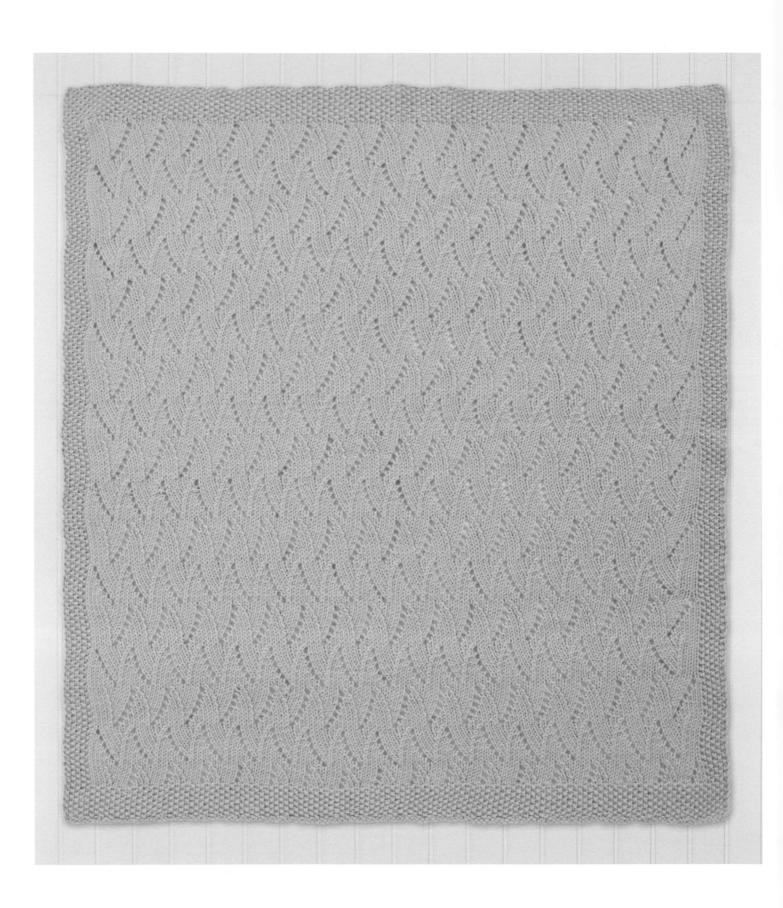

Row 18: K3, *yo, k3, k2tog, k2; rep from * across, end k1.
Row 20: K4, *yo, k2, k2tog, k3; rep from * across.
Row 22: K5, *yo, k1, k2tog, k4; rep from * across, end last rep k3.
Row 24: K6, *yo, k2tog, k5; rep from * across, end last rep k3.
Rep Rows 1–24 for pat.

Seed St (odd number of sts)
Row 1: K1, *p1, k1; rep from * across.
Row 2: Purl the knit sts and knit the purl sts.
Rep Row 2 for pat.

Pattern Note
Blanket is worked back and forth; a circular needle is used to accommodate the large number of stitches—do not join.

Blanket
Cast on 107 (135) sts.

Work in seed st for 1½ inches, ending with a WS row.

Next row (RS): Work 6 sts in established seed st, place marker, work next 95 (123) sts in Swirl Lace pat, place marker, work 6 sts in established seed st.

Work even in established pats until piece measures approx 28½ (34½) inches, ending with a WS row.

Work in seed st on all sts for 1½ inches.

Bind off.

Finishing
Weave in ends. Block to measurements. ●

STITCH KEY
☐ K
◹ Ssk
◯ Yo
◸ K2tog

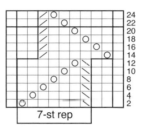

7-st rep

SWIRL LACE
Note: Chart shows RS rows only; purl all WS rows.

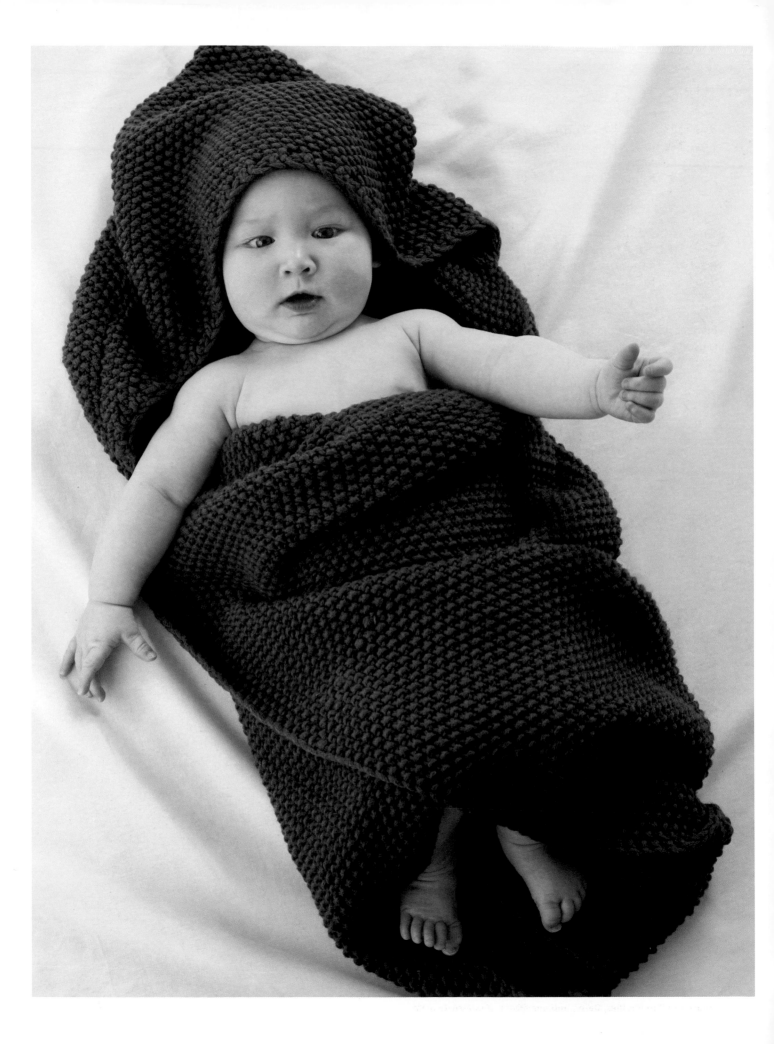

Hooded Blanket

When baby needs to be a little cozier, try this blanket with a built-in hood. It is worked in simple garter stitch throughout.

Skill Level
■□■□□ EASY

Finished Size
34 inches square

Materials
- Berroco Comfort Chunky (chunky weight; 50% superfine nylon/ 50% superfine acrylic; 150 yds/100g per skein): 5 skeins Aegean Sea #5753
- Size 10½ (6.5mm) 29-inch circular needle or size needed to obtain gauge

Gauge
14 sts and 23 rows = 4 inches/10cm in seed st.

To save time, take time to check gauge.

Pattern Stitch
Seed St (odd number of sts)
Row 1: *K1, p1; rep from * to last st, k1.
Row 2: Knit the purl sts and purl the knit sts.
Rep Row 2 for pat.

Pattern Note
Blanket is worked back and forth; a circular needle is used to accommodate the large number of stitches—do not join.

Blanket

Cast on 119 sts.

Work in seed st until piece measures 34 inches.

Bind off.

Hood

Cast on 55 sts.

Row 1 (RS): Ssk, work in seed st to last 2 sts, k2tog—53 sts.

Row 2: Work even in seed st.

Rep Rows 1 and 2 until 1 st rem.

Fasten off.

Finishing

Align hood in corner of blanket and sew in place.

Weave in ends. Block lightly. ●

General Information

Abbreviations & Symbols

[ ] work instructions within brackets as many times as directed

( ) work instructions within parentheses in the place directed

** repeat instructions following the asterisks as directed

* repeat instructions following the single asterisk as directed

" inch(es)

approx approximately
beg begin/begins/beginning
CC contrasting color
ch chain stitch
cm centimeter(s)
cn cable needle
dec decrease/decreases/ decreasing
dpn(s) double-point needle(s)
g gram(s)
inc increase/increases/increasing

k knit
k2tog knit 2 stitches together
kwise knitwise
LH left hand
m meter(s)
M1 make one stitch
MC main color
mm millimeter(s)
oz ounce(s)
p purl
pat(s) pattern(s)
p2tog purl 2 stitches together
psso pass slipped stitch over
pwise purlwise
rem remain/remains/remaining
rep(s) repeat(s)
rev St st reverse stockinette stitch
RH right hand
rnd(s) rounds
RS right side
skp slip, knit, pass slipped stitch over—1 stitch decreased

sk2p slip 1, knit 2 together, pass slipped stitch over the knit 2 together—2 stitches decreased
sl slip
sl 1kwise slip 1 knitwise
sl 1pwise slip 1 purlwise
sl st slip stitch(es)
ssk slip, slip, knit these 2 stitches together—a decrease
st(s) stitch(es)
St st stockinette stitch
tbl through back loop(s)
tog together
WS wrong side
wyib with yarn in back
wyif with yarn in front
yd(s) yard(s)
yfwd yarn forward
yo (yo's) yarn over(s)

Skill Levels

BEGINNER

Beginner projects for first-time knitters using basic stitches. Minimal shaping.

EASY

Easy projects using basic stitches, repetitive stitch patterns, simple color changes and simple shaping and finishing.

INTERMEDIATE

Intermediate projects with a variety of stitches, mid-level shaping and finishing.

EXPERIENCED

Experienced projects using advanced techniques and stitches, detailed shaping and refined finishing.

Standard Yarn Weight System
Categories of yarn, gauge ranges, and recommended needle sizes

Yarn Weight Symbol & Category Names	0 LACE	1 SUPER FINE	2 FINE	3 LIGHT	4 MEDIUM	5 BULKY	6 SUPER BULKY
Type of Yarns in Category	Fingering 10-Count Crochet Thread	Sock, Fingering, Baby	Sport, Baby	DK, Light Worsted	Worsted, Afghan, Aran	Chunky, Craft, Rug	Super Chunky, Roving
Knit Gauge Range* in Stockinette Stitch to 4 inches	33–40 sts**	27–32 sts	23–26 sts	21–24 sts	16–20 sts	12–15 sts	6–11 sts
Recommended Needle in Metric Size Range	1.5–2.25mm	2.25–3.25mm	3.25–3.75mm	3.75–4.5mm	4.5–5.5mm	5.5–8mm	8mm and larger
Recommended Needle U.S. Size Range	000 to 1	1 to 3	3 to 5	5 to 7	7 to 9	9 to 11	11 and larger

* GUIDELINES ONLY: The above reflect the most commonly used gauges and needle sizes for specific yarn categories.

** Lace weight yarns are usually knitted on larger needles and hooks to create lacy, openwork patterns. Accordingly, a gauge range is difficult to determine. Always follow the gauge stated in your pattern.

Inches Into Millimeters & Centimeters
All measurements are rounded off slightly.

inches	mm	cm	inches	cm	inches	cm	inches	cm
⅛	3	0.3	5	12.5	21	53.5	38	96.5
¼	6	0.6	5½	14	22	56.0	39	99.0
⅜	10	1.0	6	15.0	23	58.5	40	101.5
½	13	1.3	7	18.0	24	61.0	41	104.0
⅝	15	1.5	8	20.5	25	63.5	42	106.5
¾	20	2.0	9	23.0	26	66.0	43	109.0
⅞	22	2.2	10	25.5	27	68.5	44	112.0
1	25	2.5	11	28.0	28	71.0	45	114.5
1¼	32	3.2	12	30.5	29	73.5	46	117.0
1½	38	3.8	13	33.0	30	76.0	47	119.5
1¾	45	4.5	14	35.5	31	79.0	48	122.0
2	50	5.0	15	38.0	32	81.5	49	124.5
2½	65	6.5	16	40.5	33	84.0	50	127.0
3	75	7.5	17	43.0	34	86.5		
3½	90	9.0	18	46.0	35	89.0		
4	100	10.0	19	48.5	36	91.5		
4½	115	11.5	20	51.0	37	94.0		

Knitting Basics

Cast-On

Leaving an end about an inch long for each stitch to be cast on, make a slip knot on the right needle.

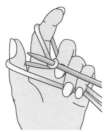

Place the thumb and index finger of your left hand between the yarn ends with the long yarn end over your thumb, and the strand from the skein over your index finger. Close your other fingers over the strands to hold them against your palm. Spread your thumb and index fingers apart and draw the yarn into a "V."

Place the needle in front of the strand around your thumb and bring it underneath this strand. Carry the needle over and under the strand on your index finger.

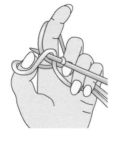

Draw through loop on thumb.

Drop the loop from your thumb and draw up the strand to form a stitch on the needle.

Repeat until you have cast on the number of stitches indicated in the pattern. Remember to count the beginning slip knot as a stitch.

Cable Cast-On

This type of cast-on is used when adding stitches in the middle or at the end of a row.

Make a slip knot on the left needle. Knit a stitch in this knot and place it on the left needle. Insert the right needle between the last two stitches on the left needle. Knit a stitch and place it on the left needle. Repeat for each stitch needed.

Knit (k)

Insert tip of right needle from front to back in next stitch on left needle.

Bring yarn under and over the tip of the right needle.

Pull yarn loop through the stitch with right needle point.

Slide the stitch off the left needle. The new stitch is on the right needle.

Purl (p)

With yarn in front, insert tip of right needle from back to front through next stitch on the left needle.

Bring yarn around the right needle counterclockwise. With right needle, draw yarn back through the stitch.

Slide the stitch off the left needle. The new stitch is on the right needle.

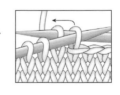

Bind-Off

Binding off (knit)

Knit first two stitches on left needle. Insert tip of left needle into first stitch worked on right needle and pull it over the second stitch and completely off the needle.

Knit the next stitch and repeat. When one stitch remains on right needle, cut yarn and draw tail through last stitch to fasten off.

Binding off (purl)

Purl first two stitches on left needle. Insert tip of left needle into first stitch worked on right needle and pull it over the second stitch and completely off the needle.

Purl the next stitch and repeat. When one stitch remains on right needle, cut yarn and draw tail through last stitch to fasten off.

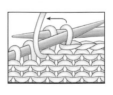

Increase (inc)

Two stitches in one stitch

Knit increase (kfb)

Knit the next stitch in the usual manner, but don't remove the stitch from the left needle. Place right needle behind left needle and knit again into the back of the same stitch. Slip original stitch off left needle.

Purl increase (pfb)

Purl the next stitch in the usual manner, but don't remove the stitch from the left needle. Place right needle behind left needle and purl again into the back of the same stitch. Slip original stitch off left needle.

Invisible Increase (M1)

There are several ways to make or increase one stitch.

Make 1 with Left Twist (M1L)

Insert left needle from front to back under the horizontal loop between the last stitch worked and next stitch on left needle.

With right needle, knit into the back of this loop.

To make this increase on the purl side, insert left needle in same manner and purl into the back of the loop.

Make 1 with Right Twist (M1R)

Insert left needle from back to front under the horizontal loop between the last stitch worked and next stitch on left needle.

With right needle, knit into the front of this loop.

To make this increase on the purl side, insert left needle in same manner and purl into the front of the loop.

Make 1 with Backward Loop over the right needle

With your thumb, make a loop over the right needle.

Slip the loop from your thumb onto the needle and pull to tighten.

Make 1 in top of stitch below

Insert tip of right needle into the stitch on left needle one row below.

Knit this stitch, then knit the stitch on the left needle.

Decrease (dec)

Knit 2 together (k2tog)

Put tip of right needle through next two stitches on left needle as to knit. Knit these two stitches as one.

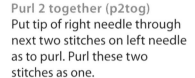

Purl 2 together (p2tog)

Put tip of right needle through next two stitches on left needle as to purl. Purl these two stitches as one.

Slip, Slip, Knit (ssk)

Slip next two stitches, one at a time, as to knit from left needle to right needle.

Insert left needle in front of both stitches and knit them together.

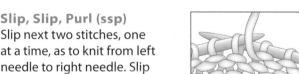

Slip, Slip, Purl (ssp)

Slip next two stitches, one at a time, as to knit from left needle to right needle. Slip these stitches back onto left needle keeping them twisted. Purl these two stitches together through back loops.

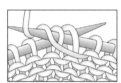
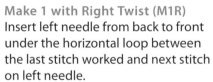

Kitchener Stitch

This method of weaving with two needles is used for the toes of socks and flat seams. To weave the edges together and form an unbroken line of stockinette stitch, divide all stitches evenly onto two knitting needles—one behind the other. Thread yarn into tapestry needle. Hold needles with wrong sides together and work from right to left as follows:

Step 1:
Insert tapestry needle into first stitch on front needle as to purl. Draw yarn through stitch, leaving stitch on knitting needle.

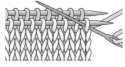

Step 1

Step 2:
Insert tapestry needle into the first stitch on the back needle as to purl. Draw yarn through stitch and slip stitch off knitting needle.

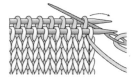

Step 2

Step 3:
Insert tapestry needle into the next stitch on same (back) needle as to knit, leaving stitch on knitting needle.

Step 3

Step 4:
Insert tapestry needle into the first stitch on the front needle as to knit. Draw yarn through stitch and slip stitch off knitting needle.

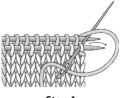

Step 4

Step 5:
Insert tapestry needle into the next stitch on same (front) needle as to purl. Draw yarn through stitch, leaving stitch on knitting needle.

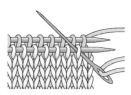

Step 5

Repeat Steps 2 through 5 until one stitch is left on each needle. Then repeat Steps 2 and 4. Fasten off. Woven stitches should be the same size as adjacent knitted stitches.

Single Crochet (sc)

Insert the hook in the second chain through the center of the V. Bring the yarn over the hook from back to front.

Draw the yarn through the chain stitch and onto the hook.

Again bring yarn over the hook from back to front and draw it through both loops on hook.

For additional rows of single crochet, insert the hook under both loops of the previous stitch instead of through the center of the V as when working into the chain stitch.

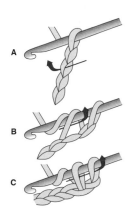

Single Crochet

I-Cord

Use 2 double-point needles. Cast on (backward-loop method) number of sts indicated. *Knit across. Do not turn. Slip sts to other end of needle. Repeat from * until I-cord is desired length. Bind off or thread yarn through sts to end.

About the Designer

Amy Polcyn has been designing professionally since 2005. Her work appears regularly in major knitting magazines and in yarn company pattern collections. She loves designing projects that are simple to knit with an interesting twist, such as cables, unusual construction or a bit of colorwork. In addition to designing, Amy works as a technical editor for yarn companies, magazines and independent designers. Prior to casting off her day job for a full-time career in fiber, she worked for 10 years as an elementary school teacher in a school for gifted students. Amy lives in suburban Detroit with her husband of 16 years, 11-year-old daughter and two wool-loving cats. In her spare time, Amy enjoys belly dancing, running and spending as much time as possible with her spinning wheel. Amy's first book, *Knit a Dozen Plus Slippers*, was also published by House of White Birches.

Photo Index

9

4

12

15

19

23

29

25

33

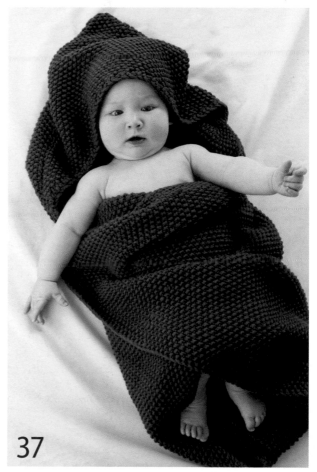

37

HOUSE of
WHITE
BIRCHES
PUBLISHERS
SINCE 1947

Baby Nouveau: Stylish Blankets for Baby is published by DRG, 306 East Parr Road, Berne, IN 46711. Printed in USA.
Copyright © 2011 DRG. All rights reserved. This publication may not be reproduced in part or in whole without written permission
from the publisher.

RETAIL STORES: If you would like to carry this pattern book or any other DRG publications, visit DRGwholesale.com.

Every effort has been made to ensure that the instructions in this pattern book are complete and accurate. We cannot, however, take
responsibility for human error, typographical mistakes or variations in individual work. Please visit AnniesCustomerCare.com to check
for pattern updates.

ISBN: 978-1-59217-339-6

1 2 3 4 5 6 7 8 9